I Hope you like books about nature. The woman who drew these pictures is a friend of mine. Merry Christmas Love Suzanne + Gregg

WILD FOX

DOWN EAST BOOKS · CAMDEN MAINE

Wild Fox

A TRUE STORY BY CHERIE MASON

ILLUSTRATIONS BY

JO ELLEN MCALLISTER

STAMMEN

FOR KEN

WHO SHARED
IT ALL

CHERIE

FOR TOM

WHO STEPPED BACK SO THAT
I COULD STEP FORWARD

JoEllen

The steel-jaw leghold trap is a barbaric and cruel device that is outlawed in over eighty nations of the world. It is the hope of those who created this book that one day soon its use will be banned throughout the United States as well.

A shorter version of this story was published in the August 1988 issue of *Cricket* magazine.

STORY © 1993 BY CHERIE MASON
ILLUSTRATIONS © 1993 BY JoEllen McAllister Stammen

COVER AND BOOK DESIGN BY LURELLE CHEVERIE

ISBN 0-89272-659-8

LIBRARY OF CONGRESS CONTROL NUMBER: 2004103205

PRINTED IN CHINA THROUGH FOUR COLOUR IMPORTS

1   3   5   6   4   2

Down East Books
Camden, Maine
www.downeastbooks.com

WILD FOX

Have you ever touched the nose of a wild red fox?

I have.

Here's how it happened. I live on Deer Isle off the coast of Maine. Red foxes also live on the island, but it's not often that you get to see one. So it was a happy surprise one summer day to find a fox pup sitting in the middle of my strawberries, calmly chomping, looking right at me. I called softly, "Hi, there! And what do you think you're doing?"

The little fox continued nibbling, dipped down for another juicy berry, and trotted off. There was something about his face that stuck in my mind.

ix months later, when that berry patch was buried under dazzling February snow, I happened to look out my kitchen window and was totally startled to see what looked like a broad orange crayon mark against the white. It was a lean red fox standing on his hind legs, reaching up toward a hanging birch log studded with suet for the woodpeckers.

Of course, I was delighted to see a wild animal out in the open during the daytime. But as I looked more closely, I winced. The fox's right front leg was nearly severed above the small black foot. I had seen steel-jaw leghold traps, but this was the first time I had seen their cruel work. Inch by inch, hour after hour, this poor young fox must have struggled to wrench his leg from the powerful grip of a trap.

Some chicken for our dinner lay defrosting on the kitchen counter. Quickly I grabbed a drumstick and ran outside. The fox bounded off in a three-legged hobble, so I put the food down on the ground and went back into the house to watch. After about ten minutes he cautiously returned, devoured the chicken, and limped off into the woods. Seeing his inquisitive, handsome face reminded me of the summer pup. I was pretty sure this was the

same fox. I waited and watched all day for him to return, but darkness came, and no fox.

The next morning, when I made my usual trip to fill the bird feeders with a bucket of sunflower seeds, I sensed someone behind me. I turned slowly; there was the fox. Crouching low, to make myself shorter and smaller and maybe less frightening, I spoke to him in a soft voice of my sympathy and concern. But that seemed to make him nervous, so I backed away. He waited, watching me steadily with his bright eyes. Holding my breath and moving in slow motion, I went inside for more chicken. Back out I came, put down the food, and carefully moved away. After a few starts and stops, the fox approached and ate. He held his hurt leg high off the ground, and I could see the bare bone that connected the foot to the leg. I imagined his pain.

A couple of days went by without another visit from the fox. I worried that his leg had become infected. Maybe he'd been run over. Winter was at its most bitter now, and the wind howled around the corners of our snug house.

Then, very early one morning, as I looked from the bedroom window to see why the crows were making such a racket, there he was. As soon as I saw him, I realized how much I'd missed him. Flying down the stairs, I grabbed some "fox food" and ran outside in that icy weather, not even caring that I was still in my pajamas.

Every morning for the next few days it was the same. The fox would wait under the suet log until I appeared with chicken and a few kind words. He would always hang back until I left, and then gulp down the free meal and hobble off. Was it my imagination, or did he look stronger? I wondered whether I should be doing more to help him. I phoned a biologist friend, who said I was right to be putting out food to help the fox regain his strength, but he warned me not to get too close because any animal in pain is unpredictable. One morning I saw that the dangling foot was gone—he'd probably bitten it off.

I now kept a special bag of chicken legs and various leftovers in the fridge

just for the fox! I started to read everything I could about foxes, and I learned that they are amazing animals. For example, they've been around for thirty million years—ten times longer than humans—and they inhabit almost every corner of the world. When they want to, red foxes can run up to thirty miles an hour, and their hearing is so keen that they can locate a tiny mouse under two feet of snow.

Fourteen drumsticks later, the fox had become such a part of my life that I decided to give him a name. *Vixen* is the word for a female fox, and even though he

was a male, I thought "Vicky" suited this shy, delicate animal perfectly. Not that Vicky cared—although I used his name over and over, he never seemed to get the idea.

Like all red foxes, Vicky had smart black ears, amber eyes, and a long, sensitive nose. Foxes use their noses to dig with, and for Vicky, who no longer could dig with his two front feet, his nose was a real lifesaver.

Vicky was about the size of a small dog. I guessed that he weighed no more than fifteen pounds. What really made him stand out was his glorious tail—almost as long as his body, and ending in a white tip. American Indians believed the tip is white because it sweeps through the deep snow, erasing the fox's tracks. This great tail makes even the coldest night bearable because a fox can simply curl up out of the wind and wrap that warm, fluffy plume over its face.

Vicky had been coming every day for over two weeks on some secret schedule, but he was edgy and always kept one eye on the forest road as he ate. I looked where he looked, but I couldn't see anything. About this time he began to tolerate my presence. I didn't have to leave after bringing out his food. Each day I was able to get just a bit closer by sometimes crouching or sometimes simply sitting quietly on the grass. Finally, after about a week of this I got so close I'd hold out a choice snack to see if he'd take it from my hand. He wanted to, I know. I could see him strain against the instinctive fear that held him on an invisible leash. But he could not ignore the warnings deep in his bones.

Spring seems to arrive in Maine overnight, as though the crocuses had been blooming under the snow all winter and were just waiting for the warm sun to roll back the covers. Each day the earth blossomed with more and more color. In comic contrast, Vicky's spectacular flame-red fur became duller and drabber as he shed his winter coat, until he turned into a scruffy little collie you wouldn't look at twice.

By April the news was out about the tame three-legged fox down at the Masons'. The UPS driver nearly hit a tree the first time he saw a fox lying in our driveway. Neighbors dropped by for a look, and an artist friend came to make some sketches. Vicky became a celebrity. The fact that he didn't run away from all this attention charmed his audience, but it began to bother me. Had he lost his healthy fear of humans? Had I harmed him by teaching him to be so trusting? I tried to ignore him, even tried to chase him away, but he would tilt his head, study me with those golden eyes, and I was a goner.

It was May. The stump of Vicky's leg had healed completely, and he certainly acted fit, often putting on quite a show. One trick was to leap to a tremendous height and come down on a real or imagined mouse. He would pounce again and again, and finally flop absolutely flat out from tail tip to muzzle.

One day he arrived limping more than usual. There was a nasty gash like
a bite on his left flank. (Vicky defending his territory? Vicky competing for a
mate?) Not too many days later, to my amazement, two larger red foxes slowly
came out of the woods, stopped at the bird feeders to cadge a few fallen seeds,

and swiftly went off again. And then, on a quiet afternoon, out of the blue,

another fox appeared and coaxed Vicky to play. The two of them jumped in the

air, nose to nose, and then fell into mock chases. The fact that Vicky had only

three feet didn't seem to dampen his enthusiasm, and it didn't look as though the other fox minded a bit that he or she was playing with a crippled companion. For half an hour they romped, the visiting fox mimicking every move Vicky made. Later I watched them both down in the cove, jumping and chasing along the beach as their tawny coats blurred in the setting sun.

ow I had even more to think about. Perhaps Vicky had found a mate. Remembering that foxes use burrows or natural gullies for dens, I decided to show him a small, well-concealed cave I had discovered. I thought it might come in handy for future fathering, since I'd learned that male foxes share in raising the pups. Knowing how he loved peanuts in the shell, I took a handful and made a peanut path to tempt him down a steep, mossy trail to the perfect fox nursery. When we got there, I continued talking softly, trying to get him to examine the den for himself. Instead, he grew suspicious, then puzzled, and finally bored. He trotted off, leaving me standing there feeling quite silly.

here was a lot about Vicky that reminded me of a cat we once had. Indeed, I read that red foxes are almost more like cats than dogs. They have catlike whiskers; their teeth are long and sharp; they stalk their prey belly-down, like a cat; and when they're angry or threatened they arch their backs and make their fur stand on end. Even the pupils of a red fox's eyes are shaped like a cat's, maybe the better to see in the dark. And finally, newborn foxes are often referred to as kits, even though they belong to the *canid*, or dog, family.

uring the peaceful days of early summer, Vicky would curl up under a big spruce, watching the house and the bird feeders, sometimes dropping off into a quick snooze while a flock of mourning doves kept a safe distance. He would rather lie down than stand, it

seemed—maybe his three good legs were still not used to the extra weight. It got so that I hated to leave for the mail or groceries because it meant leaving him. Twice I came home in the car to find him lying against the garage door, just waiting. Whenever I took a pail of scraps to the compost bin, Vicky would tag along in a half-trot, half-limp, a safe distance behind me. And when I put in raised garden beds for potatoes, he treated them as beds indeed, rolling around in the loam for a refreshing dirt bath. When I stopped to do a bit of weeding, this wild fox would stretch out on the grass not far away, completely relaxed, with his back to me. I had never before seen a wild animal do such a thing.

 ometimes he'd hang around most of the day, while on other days he'd appear about five o'clock just to look things over. As dusk fell, he always disappeared into the evening shadows. I wondered where he spent the nights. The answer came late one starry evening when I went outside with a flashlight to check the herbs for slugs. Suddenly and silently, Vicky came out of the darkness to see what I was up to. A few nights later, when

a group of us were out watching

the rippling pink and lavender

curtains of the northern lights,

who should appear to perform

his whole bag of tricks, from

mouse leap to a full somersault!

It is said that red foxes will eat almost anything. They relish little meadow voles most of all, then come field mice, grasshoppers and other insects, frogs, snakes, rabbits, squirrels, and every berry that grows. Like all predators, foxes have to take what they can get, alive or dead.

icky's menu, of course, was another matter. He finally came right up to the kitchen screen door and looked in, once he figured out that this was where his adored blueberry muffins, swiss cheese — and sometimes even leftover lobster — came from. He would chomp on these treats with eyes closed and nose pointed heavenward in total ecstasy.

At first I worried that he wouldn't be able to capture his own food again, until I watched him in the blink of an eye grab a fearless, foolish squirrel that had come too close. Another time, I caught the last inch of a mouse tail as it disappeared under his nose. He was still very much a wild fox. That made what was about to happen doubly exciting.

It was a fine summer day. I had washed my hair and was sitting out in the

sun to let it dry. Vicky was nearby.
Without thinking, I held out a
peanut that I had in my pocket,
as I had done so many times
before with no effect. He hobbled
over to me and — took it! He
took it from my hand! He took it
gently, with no snapping or
snatching. The small, sharp teeth
barely brushed my fingers.
Suddenly our eyes were inches
apart, each face studying the other.
It was at that moment that I
dared to stroke his small, slender
nose. It was just for an instant,
but the thrill of that touch
charged through me.

Then, in late August,
everything seemed to change.

Vicky was gone for a few days, and when he emerged from the woods the next time, his attitude was all business. His coat had turned back to reddish-orange and grown thick again, his tail once more a luxuriant flag. His long, thin legs looked like ink-black boots, making the shorter one less conspicuous. Amid all this splendor I saw a fresh, raw wound on his neck where the fur was torn away. Now, as in the beginning, he ate in big gulps, darting nervous glances toward the road.

We had come full circle. I realized that in all of our months together, I had never heard Vicky's voice. The typical yaps, howls, barks, screeches, and yells of red foxes did not sound here. Vicky was both silent and solitary.

Then he was gone again for three endless weeks. I imagined every kind of accident or injury until my biologist friend explained that, after their first year, male foxes leave their birthplace to establish their own territory, which can be miles away. Vicky's time had come. I sadly accepted the fact that I would never see him again.

But then, on one of the ripest days in late September, when puffs of fireweed seed floated on the air and the North Atlantic was as still as a great pond, there he was. I was so overjoyed that I stumbled over my own feet in my rush to get him something to eat. But for the first time since I'd known him, Vicky turned up his nose at a handout, and a blueberry muffin at that.

"Good," I said. "You like what you can catch much better." He didn't
need me anymore.

Vicky wouldn't settle down and was obviously fearful of something in the
direction of the road. So this time *I* followed *him* as he trotted on his three good

legs to the other side of the house. There he lay down in his fox-curl not more

than six feet away from me.

I sat on the doorstep and told him how much I loved his visits. I told him

how he must not think that all humans were on his side. And, most important, I

31 🐾

warned him to be very, very careful during the long and dangerous fur-trapping season ahead. I told him other things, too. After a bit, my gentle friend slowly got up and, without a backward look, limped out of sight.

I sat for a long time.

The name for fox in French folklore is *Reynard*, which means "unconquerable through his cleverness."

"May it be so, my Vicky," I whispered.